DANCERS ARE POEMS

By this author

Dancer and Spectator: An Aesthetic Distance
Dancer and Other Aesthetic Objects
Dancers Are Poems

Dancers
Are
Poems

James Michael Friedman

Balletmonographs

San Francisco

Library of Congress Catalog Card Number: 83-71533

Balletmonographs, 2545 Pomeroy Court
South San Francisco, California 94080, U.S.A.

International Standard Book Number 0-9604232-1-4

Printed in the United States of America

for you, for me, for us

CONTENTS

DANCERS ARE POEMS

DANCING MASTER

Dehumanize the chap or lass next door.
Plasticize them. Rubberize them. Marbleize them.
Banish the habits of commonplace dreams.
Stretch their bones; break their muscles.
Fly proudly your banners of symmetry,
equilibrium, precision and discipline.
You are the teacher they'll soon hate
and in time come to adore.

AUDIENCE

As crowds at ticket windows,
as spectators in theatres,
as those who give ovation
we perish shortly thereafter.
As a public we're but a concept.
As a dancer's great public,
vaguely there yet indispensable,
we've energized a growing enclave
inside an enormously bigger world.
You and I live as a throng
far more real in the minds of dancers,
at times a prize to be won
or a horde to fear,
than in our own reckoning.

SIPPING

The image of the dancer
ferments within us, as does
fine wine in good casks.
We are left with aesthetic residues
of thoughts or feelings or moods.
Our perceptions grow to become
appreciation as we taste the wine
or perceive the dancer.

YOU AND THEY

Look not backstage for the dancer;
one merely finds a neighbor.
Attend no parties for the star;
you'll simply meet the guest.
Search no schools for heroes;
classrooms grant no favors.
Only people can be found in class,
at parties and backstage.
These are but people, athletes and friends,
frustrated fools and tormented souls
craving balance, line and form.
You and they create the dancer,
the star and soloist,
giving birth to the image on stage.

ALTERATIONS

We look.
We attend to the dancer,
not meddling, not disturbing the image.
No causes, no consequences, no meanings matter.
We absorb a quality of what is seen.
Things are things.
Then we, in an instant,
move on to amplify and imagine.

SWEAT

Threads, strips, sheets of aqua metal
glittering over brow and bone,
heart and spirit, nape and back.
Rolls of moisture,
beads of bright bits,
silos of sodium,
crystals and vapors are messy.
They damage identities of dancers
who for a moment can become
aesthetic things, while we watch
with dry necks and pits.
Comfort is our choice and we'd wish
dancers wouldn't shed gaudy tinsel
into space and across our eyes.

DISPOSABLES

Let us remove the dancer from the dance.
Why not? Today is the day of replacement.
Now what would you for them exchange?
We're off to a good start. We own
the theatre, scenery, lighting and theme.
We own programs, patrons, tickets and music.
What more is there to do but replace,
replace the dancer with something that moves.

INSULT

Yogurt and candy bar eater,
bunion-toed oddity and biped,
poverty person and stinter on luxury,
shiny glowing animal that sweats,
sweats profusely amid the poverty,
the bunions, candy and yogurt.
Your name is Dancer.
You plead your case and we, who work,
would wonder if a subsidy you'd wish
of yogurt, candy and your bunions.
Dance is not on our favors list.
Go on with your business,
bunions and candy and yogurt.
Such things we'll treat another day.

FAN LETTER REVERSED

Of two splendid words
on a gold gift medallion
a fine dancer said,
I love the engraving.
It made me laugh, but it also
touched me deeply that you
remember my performances enough
to title me, even in jest . . .

BODY

The body of the spectator can be
a dead heavy weight, a monstrosity,
a walking corpse in which one lives,
an autocratic imprisoner and judge,
an animal near the time of death,
a floundering, bumbling, stumbling beast.
Dancers carry features close to ours.
Even during their dance they build
ideals springing from our own moves.
Dancers show signs in everyday life
of wear, tear, uncertainties galore.
Then again once on stage uncertainties wane.
Living ideals supplant the time of death.
The corpse becomes an angel.

USING

We see the knife and fork, pot and pan.
Seeing them we use them;
by using them we see them.
We see dancers as nothing of use.
Art objects and mere images grasp us
and we become, as it would seem,
instruments, objects, things of use
not for us but indeed by them.

COPRODUCTION

We shuffle,
rearrange,
amplify those dancers.
Their figures are but figments
beyond those in a choreographer's head.
Your intention during moments of seeing
matches the worth of the artist, designer,
architect, composer and dance maker
during early hours of creation.
Images of dancers exist between things
and concepts, real solids and pure models,
midway between things like rock or ink or clay
and ideals not to be realized . . .
. . . enter the spectator.

ADORATION

Would you, my sensible friend,
place on pedestals those fine dancers
whose lives most personal you know not?
Would you, intelligent soul, tend to
adore and worship such plain personages?
Those people are mere people
as carpenters are carpenters; models, models;
godesses, godesses; truckers, truckers.
It is a matter of work and pay.

MEMENTO

A program concludes and curtain descends.
Having shared with dancers
allegro rhythm and adagio grace
our bodies enter a black late night.
Planets balance and whirl.
Red lights at cross walks have us pose.
Green ones set us in motion.
We enter the night and seize
the nature of some dancer.
Its mass we filter and purify,
shred it to bits,
then rebuild and magnify
our memento in the night.

WHY DANCE?

Some kids have feet that seem to point.
Many thrive on a parent's praise.
A few feel special only when in motion
and some love to work up a sweat.
Adults? There are reasons like exercise,
curing ailments, watching weight, ridding boredom,
venting energy, looking graceful, expressing stress,
and moving with music whether rock or waltz or . . .
So you too do dance, do you?

DANCE MATERIALS

nails and wood and copper
arms and noses and legs
pigments and marble and canvas
feet and fingers and teeth
cloth and tones and ink
everyday things forming everyday art.
new materials, old materials
materials from nature
affect the lives of uncommon things.
magnificent sights and sounds of art
do not suddenly erupt in full bloom.
quarried stone and nurtured youth
after much work phenomenal images become.

TUNING IN

Works of art and truly good dancers
become noticed for their rich essence
while free thinking folks choose their
items despite, by chance, no awards
or reviews or fame being sought.
You reach out to grasp those things
toward which you're naturally pulled.
A certain art object or dancer symbolizes
concretion of your own artistic intent.

UTTERANCE

You call out the name of a dancer.
There appears an invisible audible aura
framing the word that has just left your lips.
It is not the name of your neighbor,
not the term you give the grocer,
not the appellation of any dear loved one.
It is more on the order of things of the arts.
And with its enunciation there suffuses in you
thoughtfeelings of a peculiar energy.
The name of your dancer springs forth
rife with implications and meanings:
genre, era, style, value and surprise.
It is merely a simple name.

SPECTATOR POWER

Watching dancers we become giver and receiver.
We return to them what they've yielded to us.
Dancers hold only potentials of qualities.
It is for us and others to do the unveiling.
Appreciation, a mutual venture with dancers,
calls on us to administer our souls
for fashioning images of those dancers.
For they cannot call themselves art.
You and others ordain such things.

EMIGRANT

In a theatrical realm dancer and spectator entwine,
each remaining distinct save for that moment
when there evolves the temporary fusion.
Dancers instigate it; spectators fulfill it.
Our love for them allows them
to realize their instinctual need.
We validate their choreokinetic nature,
their transfiguration from sweating hunks
of moving mass to aesthetic beings.
The prior entity was only one of billions
of daily people who attempts to depart
from quotidian life, our aesthetic perception
grants the deportation.

ART SUPPLIES

Cheap materials of all the arts
become substance of fine appearance.
Building stones no longer are loose rock,
symphonic themes no longer are peasant airs,
paints and canvas no longer are preliminaries,
words from poets no longer are words from friends.
The hand, the foot, the arm, the leg, noses,
chests, behinds, heads, toes and knees
no longer are mere flesh and mass in the dance.

WEIGHT

Sprightly dancers of pure image,
performers whirling, swooshing, leaping,
a dancer's mass means nothing to us.
Those kilograms have no kilograms.
Weight never weighs a thing.
Movement, you see, is another realm.
Adagio weighs nothing, nor does allegro.
The tiniest of swift dancers
who would be ninety humanly pounds
weighs zero till you intervene
amid her well sprung leap
and are flattened to the boards.
That's an instance of weight (in motion).

AMALGAM

Dancers are composite objects of art.
Aware they are of time and force.
Possessed they be by a sense of space.
Desirous they remain to launch moments
of primal rhythm, seconds of weightlessness,
eternities of precarious balance and pause.
Kinetic needs and common folks consolidate.
Elements of the arts mesh in the human figure;
the artist and the material transform into one.

CIRCULARITY

The creation of dancers becomes
a circular affair.
Dancers give rise to spectators.
Spectators grant rise to dancers.
Both are fleeting figures
here one moment, gone the next.
Each exists like trees in nature
viewed or demolished.
We do not convey emotion
to dancers. They first stir
in us that rage we bear
that in turn
forges their image.

CHAT

Speak to me, dancer.
Tell me about ascending the air.
Speak of flight and weightlessness.
Tell of the joy of motion through space.
Comment at length about travels and theatres.
Regale me with accounts of mirth and errors made.
Mention the wombish warmth of wet warm sweat.
Dancer, speak to me!
and do it through dance.

DANCERS ARE

The rond de jambe, the pirouette, the jeté,
contraction and release, fall and recovery . . .
newer movements and modes undergo evolution.
Dancers as technical objects transform
into art objects, change from complex beings
to sheer entities of our aesthetic seeing.
With costumes, scenery, and lighting from designers,
stories from scenarists, motion from choreographers,
music by composers, the stagecraft of technicians,
dancing persons are bludgeoned away from their
secure and comfortable studios to be given chance
to metamorphose when dropped into a choreotheatrical
world of art.

BEGINNINGS

Glaring transparent glassy glass,
enormous chunks of impenetrable marble,
strong sinewy elastic human images
do issue endless prismatic radiances,
wondrous rocky riches and dreamy movements.
Yet they cannot guarantee the coming
of noble buildings, great statues or fine dancers.
They are akin to other promising resources of art
in the hands and minds of artists.

USELESSNESS

Of dimensions theatre offers three.
Paintings reveal but two.
Films show us life,
while writings stir visions.
Music monopolizes time;
architecture, great space.
Sculpture converts stone
and dance transforms us.
What is shared?
Certainly nothing practical.
No means are serving any ends.
Even by us dancers and art objects
cannot be used, only observed.

LOST CONTINENT

It was said during the time of a big depression,
the great United States depression of the 1930s,
it was said that balletic dance was a speculative
though courageous venture looked upon skeptically
since it was felt to be something foreign
to the temper and taste of
        the American People,
and generally regarded as being
        without a future.

BEAUTY

Beauty does not exist
solely about the dancer.
Sensations we feel aren't qualities
of things seen or heard.
Loveliness does not appear alone.
It is a value in our perception,
and fine dancers not perceived
are for us joys not felt.
The dancer who dances alone
is a painting hung with no patron near,
a grand building with no observer by,
music and poetry without the listener,
no beauty.

OLYMPIAN

Dancers, some fans don't know, are athletes
but appear in the arts rather than sport.
They show the speed of sprinters,
elevation of high jumpers, strength of shotputters,
and concentration of pole vaulters.
In sport the conflict, suspense and surprise,
divorced from the winning, could be theatre.
Those athletes can reveal a beauty of motion,
elegance in action.

COMPOSER

Thirty-eight bars of somber drama
suggestive of trials and tribulations forthcoming,
fourteen bars to follow so the viewer
will feel some respite, too, is in the offing.
Then let us be transported through an auditory maze
allowing a myriad of ideas and dreams and thoughts,
all manners and forms of spirit and mood,
to direct our beings and bearings abroad
through a narrative as disruptive and complex
as the era in which we struggle to know . . . . .
"Give me next a violent brassy
and crashing tympanic seven measures,"
demands the choreographer of a composer.

RECALLING

We return after long absence
to a choreosphere for contemplating
one who long ago had steps so quick,
body swift, legs strong, arms gentle.
It was memories of some dancer's vibrancy
and feelings replete with verve
like strong tea or bright dawn.
Free from gravity your spirit soars.
Somewhere in you a chant begins.
Somewhere in you there's a primordial grin.

CHOREOGRAPHER

Angrily a hand tossed a chair across a stage,
suggestively one body gently led the other,
arrogantly an eye cast the proper answer,
graciously some fingers pointed the direction,
harshly a distant voice shouted the steps,
mutually a pair of feet solved the problem.
They come in all manners of artistic frames,
they give birth to dance through notes or without,
they form it as despots or create with others,
they rule the roost or they share the domain.
The work founders or the work succeeds,
the public yawns or the public cheers!

FINDING

All media sway our feelings
deeming who we should like,
and the great-man theory of history
bids us to look towards stars beyond.
Greatness is stardom pushing us to pick
illustrious persons who've been hyped.
But scan the stage to see who's dancing
beside those famed much touted stars.
It's like picking a poem all by yourself.
Something dormant inside you awakens NOW.

STAGEHAND

What you've seen could fill a book
of wonders and mirth and joy.
But tragedies and deaths you've also seen
on the boards of great Terpsichore's stage.
Way back there and on far sides
do you see what we see out front?
Work is work and art is art.
Sweaty dancers and veneer props
don't make for huge events.
Yet I'd prefer to think you too
see your dreams, and a fine dancer
once human turns kinetic work of art.

ACCLAIM

The dancer as a wonder of art grows viable
in the realm of your most private
passions and interests.
Epic poems and splendid statues remain
inane things until expanded
beyond objecthood.
Exceeding the fame of a public thing
is its place in your own world.
Outstanding art works and masterful dancers
only gain renown in your own heart.

SCENARIST'S LAMENT

Now your fortunes are but rubble.
Try, we dare, to write a *Giselle,*
or on misty lakes with swans fluffy white.
How 'bout war among mice or a Sugarplum Fairy
who can lead the way to marvelous lands?
Write, if you will, of noble deeds and
castles and a princess who'll come awake.
Try to tell of toy makers and mechanical dolls.
Old scenarist, you've done all you could.
A new age of dance has long arrived
and with it new glories and prides,
a day of abstraction.

US

We see gorgeous objects of nature,
the rocks, the leaves, the autumn,
beach shells, rainbows and textures of trees.
In the arts we see forms and colors,
lines and angles, stone, bronze, glass,
wood and clay and paint. We see
hair and skin, colors of our forms,
lines and angles of our muscles and bones,
the structures and patterns of our own kind,
we from nature amidst the arts who dance.

COSTUMER

Once they commissioned you to build costumes like buildings.
Stunning jewel adorned and cloth rich they were.
Tiered layers and colors of rainbows they shown
like masterpieces, for indeed each was that.
When hem lines went up and fleshy ankles glowed
you, the costumer, commenced your new work.
What have we now but leotards and tights,
and that in some circles is pretentious enough.
For dance nudity is natural and costumery affected.
But occasionally one argues the point
of the beautiful versus the commonplace,
and we would hunger for the old costumer.

THINGS IN NATURE

There are special objects of nature,
the mountains, dancers and rivers
that win our gaze for their
unique essence and image.
They serve no end, but
culminate in a finale themselves.
Their lives are the terminations
of quests of spectators
who would seek things in nature
turned aesthetic.

SCENERY

Last month we saw colorful scrims hanging upstage right.
A week ago textured somber drapery hung downstage left.
Yesterday it was a wiry rather bare configuration
spanning thinly across center stage among the dancers.
Such are contrasts to that enormous and noble scenery
of forests and glens, lakes and ponds, homes and castles
given to stages centuries ago for those big big ballets.
My, my, how beautiful and grandiose they all were.
Night after night the wealthy patrons viewed them.
Today our imagination roams across sparse scenery
generating in our souls the moods, feelings, thoughts
which grand paintings of fabled lands did not allow.

COINCIDENCE

Tear away your brother and sister
from images of the dancer.
In theatres you're at museums and galleries,
not pubs or stadia or sport arenas.
You watch paintings and porcelains
but dancers, too, come from muses.
No mock, no copies, no friends
or relatives next door are they.
By chance they bear arms and legs,
heads and toes and all that we know.

MASS TIMES WEIGHT

Walk on stage during performance.
You are showered with sweat,
bumped, bruised, sworn at.
Hugely heavy hulks aren't dancers,
only people of pounds and size,
humans weighed and measured.
Aesthetic creations become diluted
when measurements become known.
These are friends and kin, not dancers.
Aesthetic things don't crunch bones.
Dancers are kinetic images
till . . . CRASH.

PROPRIETY

Stay away from dancers!
They are mere illusions.
There are no dancers backstage,
only duckfooted, sweat drenched people.
Musical scores are not the music.
We do not copulate with bronze statues.
We don't poke fingers through paintings
or eat long pages of delicious poems.
So, why seek the dancer
who, in our own world, does not exist . . .

ILK

We and dancers, one would suspect,
are for all time from different kinds.
Yet dreams would be shared not so diverse.
We are bound through easy liaison,
one of us perceiving, the other experiencing,
in the pith of dance to share dreams of a leap,
a pose, a turn, fancy feet and exuberant spins;
both seeking weightlessness, such agility,
so rare an elegance, the vivacity of dance
with visions of mellifluous adagio or sights
of swift allegro. Spectator and dancer remain
two sorts though sharing dreams not so diverse.

SKEINS

A dancer is seen in various ways
by spectator, agent, or wife,
stage manager, producer, or friend,
lighting tech, costumer, and fan,
set designer, composer, and uncle,
choreographer, doorkeeper, or pal.
All have their skeins.
Images of the dancer change.
It is not as dancers are
but as to us they appear.

SHATTERING

Ceaseless ovation . . . curtain descending . . .
. . . rising . . . coming down again . . . up once more . . .
Strange strong confident dancers
comfortable and secure with makeup,
possibly confused and shy without.
Virtuoso dancer of magic and magnetism
surprisingly becomes so very much smaller,
almost frail in her clothes of the street.
Devotees of great dancers have cooled
at first meeting when theatricality was lost.
Sensationally striking dancers may be seen
on first meeting meek and placid little things.

PURER

"Abstract" is a big word that applies
to many forms of dance. What we get
may be a human figure which now lives
as the denuded quantum of tension in space,
a non-named, non-nationalized kinetic integer,
something complete without story reference.
The worthiness of dance might be found
as gestures disappear. Then when least aware
we come to know those fine bodies must
bear sweat and birthdays at random.

INDEFINABLE

The dancer is limitless,
enters all music,
becomes all expressions,
assumes all forms.
Dance remains an open concept.
Arts and their objects gain new guises
from ever changing cultures and artists.
We define paint and brush, man and woman,
moons and planets and black holes,
but not art,
not dance,
not dancers.

IMPRINT

Fine dancers like fine art
transcend their own eras.
They live beyond the politics,
the economics, the ethos
of their day.
Though art objects don't die,
and dancers do,
the myths of performers may harden
like clay or become as stone.
War, plague, flood and fire do not
destroy legendary dancers
from earlier times.

GHOSTS

Long long long after some dancers
have vanished from theatrical life
their adoring fans easily resurrect
and contemplate their moving images.
Those old dancers wander from party
to party, sad and lonely figures
whose world of applause has collapsed.
Reality is not embedded in memories.
Kinetic comrades and dancing victories
hastily pursue them like ghosts,
the same ghosts that complement
the lives of adoring fans.

DUO

Two dancers reflecting one another,
mixture of classic and modern.
Choreographic shapes and designs
spun by the yarn of exhilaration.
Dancers of metalic very light blue.
Futuristic work echoing ancient forms.
Consonance then dissonance then consonance.
Coalescence of painterly and sculptural ways.
Able dancers transmute from hidden technical
beings into perceptible aesthetic entities.
Bare choreoconcepts become environments
during momentary lives of two dancers.

COMPETING

Skeletal trees surrounding us in Winter,
sounds of birds and brooks at Spring's dawn,
gorgeous puffy white clouds high in Summer blue,
and crackling red yellow leaves in Autumn
grant us sight and sound of natural things
that painters and composers might have dreamed.
Dancers, kinetic human beings forming such
a small area of nature, enter our senses.
Rainbows and dancers exist for us to view.
Those colorful arcs do it quite comfortably,
while dancers try to surpass them, and sustain
sheer havoc and near destruction to their bodies.

GRAVITY

The curse of gravity gives rise
to the spirited marvels of dance.
Without it our entrechats wouldn't be.
Dancers of such verve no more we'd see
as they'd rise higher and higher and crunch
legs fluttering and audience aghast
up through and way beyond the roof.
Leaps too would be long overruled.
Going through walls for a further mile
is not the point of graceful moves.
Give thanks to gravity in the past
for making possible the art of dance.

TRANSACTIONAL

Observer of dancers, you are not
the passive creature you thought.
You absorb the painting,
the music, the piece of sculture,
the poem; you do something with them.
You take in the dancer.
Your dancer and you do not live
at that moment so free.
That evanescent bond is not so thin.
You and your dancer become something
because each of you soon exists
by virtue of the other.

EXPECTATION

If the film is too poor,
the opera too marred,
the music tinny or
the poem ill read;
the cathedral too shattered,
the painting too dim,
a carving splattered
or the dancer inept,
art objects stay in limbo
as mere potentials. What you have
is a theatre filled with enraged people
glaring at an empty stage.

MISPLACED

Human pillars in tutus and tights some believe
are born in iron mills instead of wombs.
Yet the right man, yet the right woman,
these two merge in dance to perfuse
a volume of charisma and warmth
seldom gleaned from other arts.
We travel far for stones
to behold at museums and there
caress other pillars that wear no clothes,
bare pillars with no muscle, flesh or bone,
admiring their cold cold stone.

FATE

More than one dancer has said
quietly within, "I did not choose,
no, I did not choose this.
It happened. It happened.
And now I live with it, every minute."
A tree doesn't choose its cabinet
or a color its canvas or a word its poem.
A beam of steel selects no building
and a musical note no song.
Granite cannot deem its course
nor bronze its figures.

VALUE

Dancers exist in a middle state between
aesthetic objects and just common folk.
Performers perish as do plain things
or are exalted like works of art.
Both a dancer and the art work wane
by toll of age, fire, war and flood.
Dancers and art works are built of material
suffering the scuffs, mildew and scratches of time.
Reputations may grow far beyond their origins.
Some dead dancers crescendo in value
like fine old objects of art.

TOMORROW

Dancers exist as kinetic results
of ideal forms and types from cultures.
They come forth as readily as
hamburgers, cricket, Ming vases.
Next season we'll note shifts of interest.
Current forms and types are seen
as both the present and the past.
Yesteryear's ideals remain rare today,
and tomorrow's reality is only the vision
of farsighted crackpots and strange artists
whose music and dance serve to anger and provoke.

PREFERENCE

Few people choose their own works of art.
Fewer yet select their dancers.
Big performers like big art works
sway the horde by far flung repute.
Fame is a great and heavy imprint.
We look and listen by virtue of someone
who talks louder and clearer and whose words
we've mistaken for being engraved on tablets.
With their chisels and pens critics send
fine things down into limbo or up through
the world of art. But you must pick.

APHONIC

Choreography without the music,
indeed!
Few spectators would await such business.
But, we would wonder, need the music
reveal itself to dancers who in turn
must kinetically translate it for us?
Tempo and rhythm can be the sole property
of dancers in a musically absent movement.
Dance motion, like any aesthetic reflection,
can be seen as carrying its own
reason to be.

COHABITATION

Tempi of dancers render their own
qualities of time while we enjoy
a slow relaxed gentle adagio
or the appealing alacrity of allegro.
Implications of time arise from moving forms.
Our alignments with real clocks must be stopped
while during that space we become inhabiters
of a junction where a performer's spatial
and temporal coordinates cross. We live
for the while in a time zone tended by
creatures functioning kinetically.

DEMISE

The image of the dancer does not die
as do concrete, bronze and steel.
Images can't be burned like great books,
carved on as statues in parks,
botched like badly played sonatas,
forged as fine old paintings,
cracked to shards as befalls ancient works.
The image of the dancer remains sheer and aloof,
pure imagery till even that dissolves.
No mess. No fuss.
Nothing to clean up.

EDEN

That bright red apple glows in the day's light.
An amusing dancer dances a scherzo.
Some yellow bananas look delicious,
and a little dancer hangs from a tree
while a bush of white roses far below
reflects glitterings of morning dew.
We're enticed to bite, to pick, to pluck.
We would eat if we could, steal what we would,
fight if we might move the whole affair
to our neck of the woods
to suffer disillusion.

LIQUEUR

Savoring a drop of intense spirits,
the drop formed as small as can be
gotten on the tongue, suffusing softly
as moments elapse, an essence
expands to wider regions within you.
Becoming familiar with your chosen dancer
you've learned his or her nature
as you would a drop of liqueur,
savoring as you would your dancer's form
and movement, distilling a kinetic essence
through contemplation over time.

SLOW DANCE

Spellbound in our theatre chairs we extract
a small section from the large work of art.
With our perception we frame its own worth.
Extended passage on passage on passage
of graceful adagio dance seems an entity
distinct and complete, a work within a work.
We enter a long landscape to view
a meadow showing the briefest
natural event of place and time.
A lightly moving slowly turning dancer
glides with a partner across theatrical space.

FAST DANCE

Kinetic spirit exists neither visibly nor invisibly.
It seems an island on which dancer and observer
musically coalesce during a brief rhythmic encounter.
A section of allegro tempts us to sojourn
with dancers midst swift flows of energy.
Resonating in the mode of allegro we become
finely tuned strings plucked by vivacious dancers
of our choice.
We watch, wait, wish for the nature of vivacity.
It comes to our vision when so high a degree
of its spirited self takes form.
Dancers become allegro by the fusion
of their material beings with that universal
nonmaterial urge to dance, dance swiftly!

INTERMISSION

Yawning, stretching, ambling off to rest rooms.
Jostling, bustling, scurrying toward counters
for Irish coffees and champagne.
Glancing, staring, wending one's way
through the crowd of dresses and suits,
slacks and pants, ties and sneakers.
The colors and styles and sizes and shapes
produce a distinct show all their own.
To be forgotten, this amusing scene
gives way to the next ballet
and the crowd is no more till a roar
from grateful spectators watching dance
with keen eyes and full bladders
amble and scurry and wend their way
to repeat their very very own play.

TOMBSTONE

Remembrance—
one dancer's spatial dominance, another's grace,
a person's fleeting nature, someone's lingering aura,
one's ease and control, another's mellifluous flow,
and somebody's endless energy loom as bright basics
about which we retain kinesthetic memories.
Essential aspects of certain dancers move greatly
through your feelings and build a temporal dimension
in which we cherish entire lives of dancers.
On stone one could chisel for a fine performer,
"This person displayed enormous
athletic fortunes yet was subject
to the aural intrigues of music
and wished forever to execute
rhythmic transgressions in space."

ALLEGRO

There's a hearty taste for rapid
well spun dance offering swift feet,
soaring bodies, fleeting figures.
There's a deep felt wish to see forms,
then feel the vitality of allegro.
Dancers exist in rare relationships
to the concept of evanescence and motion.
Some virtually become visual kinetic instances
of moods or ideas or impressions.
Your choice of a dancer is something like
the music you choose which expresses you.
That dancer remains the essence of your dance.
Such fresh new exciting intangible verve!
Your spirit takes wing.
Fleeting . . . speed . . . swift . . . image . . .

SEARCHING

Dancers are not mere physical objects
though their roots reside deep, deep
down in corporeal existences of bodies.
Dancers appear when we see them purely
during movement, as images, not touchables.
At parties you go amiss seeking their names.
That is all you will find, only names.
Dancers aren't persons, just recollections.
They've no gender, no voting rights, no appetites.
Guests at parties thrashing through domestic space
seeking dancers, world acclaimed illustrious dancers,
search rooms, halls, nooks, closets, even bathrooms
and around freshly cut hedges in spacious gardens
but fail to obtain those elusive entities of the arts,
those mere recollections and simple images.

PREPARATION

Externally impelled young people float
through indecisions across alien lands.
There are no rites of passage for youth.
The tribe is gone. Industry has arrived.
Alas, there are no guides and ways.
But wait, notice the young dancer.
A rite of passage for those who follow
their need to dance bestows the course.
Internally impelled youthful dancers
glide through decisions across arduous
but astounding territories of meaning.
The pupil of dance knows the custom
and ceremony of this group within a group,
a community of terpsichoreans
amid a nation's industries.

AESTHETIC MODE

Daily clash with classic pose,
modern figures, jazz and ethnic verve
of dancers releasing feelings and forms.
You and I assist others who would in dance
wish to become moving things of art.
It is we who shift our mode of awareness
to aid performers toward their goal.
Dancers who make the transformation become
for the moment relocated imported figures
formerly of commonplaces where we too lived.
Our gaze grows fixed upon them during seconds
which demand nothing of us at anytime.
By a change of attitude we alter our perception,
saving the dancing personage from otherwise
traditional and selfish areas of our lives.

WHERE'S THE DANCER ?

Driftwood on a beach.
Art?   Perhaps not.
Driftwood hung on your wall.
Art?   Perhaps so.
Chimpanzee painting on canvas.
Art?   Depends where later it goes.
In a zoo or museum of history
the muses may not smile down.
At a gallery of paintings
then perhaps they do.
Human being dancing on a beach,
in the street, at a gallery,
in a museum, in your backyard,
at the theatre. Where does the human
become the dancer?

APPEARANCE

Dancers are not praised for their bulk.
Their motion is the subject of our gape.
Invading our senses the movements of people
collect as kinetic content in our minds.
You are not concerned about the paper pages of poetry
or ten pound weight of a book.
You do not see reels of plastic at the cinema
or black ink on scores at concert halls.
Ballets arise from a wealth of physical properties
yet reveal only transient images of dancers
who occur through a medium of motion.
Features, not substances, force us to take home
more than thoughts about fine performances.
Our souvenirs become simple residues
of the appearances of things.

CURTAIN CALL

You can't see the people,
just lights glaring from afar
streaming right into your face.
But you hear the people,
their thousands of blaring hands
streaming right into your ears.
From a distance through the dark
the ovation becomes overwhelming.
They call you and your kinetic colleagues
back, and then back, and back again.
Your exhaustion is far far overridden
by the love, the blinding lights,
the deafening roar and clapping hands.
Will they remember you next season,
when newer soloists dance for them?

SALT WATER

Huge powerful dancers,
athletes supreme.
Hair and muscle, fur and skin,
lithe supple flexible exquisitely
graceful and powerfully huge dancers.
They collapsed on the floor,
leaving watery marks symbolic
of their mortality and frailties.
They inspected their feet,
swallowed vitamins,
raised their legs above their heads,
gulped at the air and behaved
like washcloths being rung and rung
and rung, but looking more like
butter in a skillet melting.

EVANESCENT

Dancers are not made of crystal or gold,
nor of bone or muscle or blood.
Vases are crystal, rings gold, and it is we
who possess blood and muscle and bone, and look
like dancers, though dare not approach them
to chance their transformation back into us.
Dancers are spatial entities amid media of time.
Vanishing beings living to dance and dancing to live,
they are born from people who balance,
people who bend and stretch,
people who fall and rise,
people who hurt and groan,
people who quiver offstage.
Then a cue is given.
Dancers appear,
but for the instant.

IRONIC

Grandma never saw modern dance till tonight
though she lived through the '20s
and '30s in America when history
was being made.
How ironic, now she asks if this
is part of all the funny stuff
going on today among the youth.
Strange thing, she lived in New York City
during those long gone times before we were here.
We have only the history books.
She had the real thing, but missed it.
She worked in a beanery in the Village,
washed floors and walls around Park Avenue,
made love near the river,
but missed the history being made.
Grandma never saw modern dance till tonight.

WHAT'S A DANCER?

Who knows what be a dancer?
We do not circumscribe boundaries of dance.
Terpsichore is not mere analysis and concept
free from stunning human movement.
We do not talk about dance in terms
of physical limits or tired bodies.
Human bodies do not move in stark oblivion.
They glide and twirl within our view.
We create milieus as much as they.
Dance has little to do with preexisting
arms and legs; it is a matter of seeing.
We grant, as does the choreographer, its worth.
Rather than human bodies being the limits of dance
its limits, quite fluid and ever expanding,
involve circumstance and era and our perception.
Who knows what be the dancer, next?

DISGUISED

She came forth from the stage door.
Yet it was not she, but only one
who bore the same name as she.
At the stage door, entering the cool night,
she was a bit shorter, a bit smaller,
far less of a splendid creature
than the one who bore her name
onstage in all those dances.
A smiling young man came toward her
as she entered the night.
He lifted a loaded dance bag
from her arms and said something.
They went off into the night
like kids laughing.
My serious, voluptuous, womanly danseuse—
like a kid, laughing.

REVISITING

You're swimming along or jogging in the park,
riding an elevator or eating ice cream,
waiting for the bus, taking the ferry,
grooming a pet or having a smoke.
Without warning a moving image of
sparkling candescence beams inside you.
The poem is gone, the painting was seen,
some music is over or sculpture viewed,
a cathedral was bombed, a manuscript lost,
the opera was heard or ceramic cracked.
Without warning an awesome essence
of near tangible worth glows inside you.
Dancers and objects of art pass through the fog
of gone times and lost days.
That theatre or gallery inside you
flaunts its treasures beyond official hours.

THINGS OF ART

You and the Renoir canvas,
a set of verses from Frost,
or images of Isadora Duncan.
You and a Rembrandt masterpiece,
a poem by laureate Wordsworth,
or photo of a ballet dancer.
You and a chunk of Rodin,
a score by Copland,
or the body of a modern dancer.
You and a foreign film,
a Rauschenberg collage,
or some rhythmic ethnic dancer.
You, paintings and poems, cinema,
pieces of sculpture and music,
aesthetic objects found in nature,
or dancers and porcelain vases.

LOSING SOMETHING

Wars, works of art and dancers
are given to the world for attendance.
We look at them. We listen to them.
When sufficiently in attendance
we then see and hear them.
Eventually they must be lost.
A militarist loses the war.
An artist loses the work of art to the world.
The dancer yields and subsequently loses
beautiful movement to spectator and public.
Sometimes a nation does not notice a war.
Often an artist's work is not seen or heard.
When a person dances alone, is the dancer present?
Wars, works of art and dancers are meant
for audiences, publics, close friends
or merely their creators.

AGAIN

Dancers do not dance alone.
They serve the culture,
the theatre, the patron.
Music has shifted from great estates
to concert halls and the media.
Amulets of magic and sacred relics
now reside in museums and mansions.
Cameras have arrived, so have missiles and T.V.
Portraits and castles and heroic legends
no longer portray or defend or legendize.
They've been cut asunder from their origins.
And dancers, well, they can't be carried over.
Dancers remain current to the minute,
specters of the very second,
nothing lost from the past, nothing revived.
When gone, they are created anew.

FOOL

"ooohs" or "ahhhs" are heard
when some movements seem
strangely distinct from life.
The spread footed crouched dancer
ponderously shifts weight from leg to leg
ringing awe from an audience of dazzled
nonparticipants who sigh and give respectful
light intrusive touches of annoying applause.
Such would seem like the rapidity of fingers
fast and furious, to the sacrifice of music,
over keyboards during amateur events.
And of other events, one might suspect,
if a dancer were to trip and roll from stage
into orchestra pit far below we would hear
wild enthusiastic spectators applauding it well,
so so daring a feat: "oooh . . . ahhh"

CONFESSION

My date told me during intermission
how much she loves the long and strong
muscular thighs of the male dancers.
Then her eyes opened wider,
her voice grew louder,
"and those asses, those tight firm asses!"
Frowned and even scowled I did upon her.
I chided her for committing indelicacies
as an appreciator of the arts. And then
she asked me what appeals to me
about male dancers.
I told her I rarely look at them.
I adore the bodies of those females.
Their arms, their legs, their crotches,
their asses . . . . . . uhhh,
I . . . ahhhhh,

"lighting by—"

White they say is the absence of light.
Black is when the houselights go out.
And of the lighting designers, the ones who
before their names it says, "lighting by—"
well, try a red or a green or a blue,
a pink, purple, brown or gray,
try some fancy lengths of strange waves.
Try Alizarin crimson, English vermillion,
Cadmium red or instead Venetian red,
Burnt sienna or the Burnt umber,
Cadmium orange, medium; or Raw sienna,
Chrome yellow, medium; or Zinc yellow,
Zinc white or a lovely Chrome green, medium,
Emerald green, ivory black, Cobalt blue,
Cobalt violet or maybe a Manganese violet.
"lighting by—"

GALA

Searchlights brightly scanning dark sky
above the bustling opera house on this eve
as dancers stretch and jump backstage
preparing for a gigantic opening night.
Finely dressed people of much wealth
leave great autos and doff their hats
on entering the lit festive theatre.
Productions are late, dancers replaced,
lighting is faulty, sound systems raspy.
We amplify and distort beyond what could be
any reality of upcoming mirth and pleasure.
A hundred dollar ticket just to be seen
where all is seen not on stage but next to you
in the next box where others stare back
and dancers onstage are missed.
Next week during a quiet average night perhaps
a five buck ticket might grant aesthetic dreams.

TAKING THEIR PLACES

Behind a yet unraised proscenium curtain
dancers scurry about looking disheveled,
anxious, weird, uncertain, lost.
Short lines of strange shimmering figures
assemble as stagehands during final seconds
arrange props where previously planned.
Nervous human waifs smooth down wrinkles
on bright costumes in dim light.
They stretch their calves, shape their hands,
breathe deeply and bend knees for relief.
The curtain begins to rise slowly.
Sculptural beings in hanging white cloth
grace the world beneath vague moonlight glow.
Arms quietly move together through calm
followed by legs in parallel sweep across space.
Creatures originally of our sort change
to wondrously energetic romances.

PHYSICAL BODIES

The aesthetic object bears no physical self.
But the dancer has size and shape,
an inside and outside,
shares space with other things,
holds characteristics through time,
and combines qualities of color,
hardness and temperature.
That is the dancer as a body,
a plain common ordinary body.
It is what comes before something else,
something special, something of the arts.
It is what exists as being corporeal
before being set into motion
and prior to our entry in the theatre.
It is only a materiality predating
the nonphysical entity it can become.
It is the dancer's material self.

SELECTING

You listen, you look, you perceive afresh
an evening long oratorio, a gigantic cathedral,
the thousand page Russian novel or Miltonian poem,
that dominant painting spanning an entire wall,
some five story high monstrous piece of sculpture
or the panorama of a long corps de ballet.
We first see or hear great bewildering forms.
Out of your consciousness certain dancers
later arise, painterly colors, sounds and tones,
literary images, sculptural planes and angles.
We hop between totality and elements,
elements and totality, totality and elements.
Dancers merge into a moving sum,
an overall design out of which we return
to extract human entities from the greater work.
You come again to the art object to perceive,
to listen, to look, to hop back and forth.

CUE

Off in the dark dusty dreariness of the wings,
where cables like snakes wind near your feet
and lighting brackets hang ready above to decapitate,
the potential human aesthetic object—a dancer—
stands ready for the cue like a piece of sculpture
or other work of art long since arduously uncrated,
but not yet officially and ceremoniously unveiled.
In the wings the dancer waits.
The dancer awaits the cue.
People in the balcony so very high high up,
people in the orchestra terribly low to the stage,
people in the boxes peering out disdainfully,
people in the circles and stalls and tiers staring,
the conductor raises his baton and those musicians
arrange their limbs, their attentions, their eyes
for that signal when something will start.
The dancer awaits the cue;
in the wings the dancer waits.

PERSPECTIVES

You'll have to wait to be seated,
you're late.
The conductor is guarding a rare relation
between musicians and dancers
while lighting techs ready themselves
and stagehands stand by for changes.
The keyed up choreographer scans
that total production and dancers span
the length and breadth of the long deep stage.
Ticket sellers count money behind caged walls.
Food handlers set up munchies and drinks.
The influential patron eyeballs his audience
as a critic takes notes and some board member
ponders the possible worth of some dancer.
An usher anticipates the end to a solo
and quietly says in the latecomer's ear,
"I can seat you in just a minute."
Cabdrivers drive off to seek new fares.

ORIGINS

Origins of the dancer continue to be
physical things in an everyday world.
But dancers emerge from a world
uncommon to the everyday.
Theatre, the stage, dance notation,
these are nooks and crannies, the microcosms
of the big broad magnificent world of art.
Dancers as human beings and aesthetic wonders
overlap the miraculous and the commonplace.
We and they share simple beginnings.
From there we and they depart,
leaving for different provinces.
In the wings, that limbo territory,
we sense the impending shift
of a partial human figure
to a potential work of art,
the almost fellow being turning dancer
from common origins.

FLOWERS

We offer a bouquet of flowers to our dancer.

We raise a bottle of wine to the moon,

a book of verse to a countryscape,

a gold trinket to a blade of grass,

an outreach for an embrace with the sun.

All our attempts are rebuffed.

Moons don't drink,

countrysides can't read,

grass wears no gold,

suns won't hug but do scorch.

All your attempts are rebuffed.

You are but one of many lovers

of your dancer. He or she has no time

to reciprocate the flowers,

drink the wine, read any letters,

wear such gifts or return your embrace.

All our attempts are rebuffed.

We offer a bouquet of flowers to our dancer.

MIRROR

dancers living in mirrors reflecting
vain attempts toward perfect forms
of fingers and hands and arms
head and neck and torso
hips and thighs and calves
feet and toes and spirits of
dancers living in mirrors reflecting
vain attempts toward perfect forms
of fingers and hands and arms
head and neck and torso
hips and thighs and calves
feet and toes and spirits of
dancers living in mirrors reflecting
vain attempts toward perfect forms
of fingers and hands and arms
head and neck and torso
hips and thighs and calves
feet and toes and spirits of
dancers living in mirrors reflecting

COMBINATIONS

short, short, short
tall, tall, tall
square, square, square
round, round, round

angular, angular, angular
black, black, black
robust, robust, robust
yellow, yellow, yellow

jerky, jerky, jerky
brown, brown, brown
smooth, smooth, smooth
white, white, white

materials of the arts
fine physical objects
dancers as human beings
and dancers as dancers
temperaments, emotions, techniques
pigments of varied brilliance and hues
qualities of stones and timbres of tones

QUOTIDIAN

The human portion of our environment
sports blunt manners and rude mannerisms,
poorly dressed souls most ungainly,
bent frames plodding to work
down noisy morning streets,
broken frames crawling back at day's end,
obese figures in superdoopermarkets,
human power shovels furiously wolfing slop
at dull or downright hostile dinner tables
while stained mouths blow nicotine smoke.
Our human portion of the environment
sends up a cry within itself for something
beautiful and profound, something of itself
that may balance the scales and lessen the chagrin.
Much of humanity can be felt struggling
to gain a decent image of its noble
collective self through a grand art object,
piece of music, poem, piece of sculpture,
or merely a solo dancer.

WHEN IS THE DANCER ?

Notational scoring of a dance,
its premiere or mere concept,
its production in Paris or New York,
when is our aesthetic object?
Prints of a painting,
published copies of a poem,
enlargements of a negative,
when is the visually aesthetic object?
Rivulets of gorgeous language,
flowing phrases from a brook,
sterling tones from human voices,
when is the audibly aesthetic object?
Numerous bronzes from one mold,
varied renditions of a symphonic work,
three buildings from one blueprint,
when is the original work of art?
You stare and wait for the person
to become a kinetic wonder,
and it comes at rare times
as you cause its creation, yourself.

JUMP

This is not that little jump
which you did over hopscotch
when you were silly and young.
This is big serious business,
jumping for your bread and butter.
So, consider some pas couru
or a lovely glissade with its
hidden plans and latent power.
Then give us the big treat.
Stand on your left leg and cross
the right foot around to the back.
Now send your spirits to the right leg,
moving that limb around to the front
and pushing off high into the stars.
While in air swing your left leg front.
Glide through space in the grandest pose.
Do remember to keep your arms with you.
Take your choice of arabesque or attitude.
Stay up there for a seeming eternity . . . .
Stay up there . . . . . stay up . . . stay up

LIGHTING DESIGNER

Where are they? We never see them.
By candlelight, gas or incandescence
there always were lighting designers
at the world's great theatres of dance.
But what do they look like, and smell like,
and what do they eat and what do they wear?
It's become understood, so one hears,
that even casual observation indicates that
an understanding of color involves not only physics
but physiology and today of course psychology.
As a matter of simple experience a white tablecloth
appears to be just as white under candlelight
as it does under daylight, despite the fact
that the light reflected by the tablecloth
into the observer's eye is actually as yellow
as the candle flame itself. Our dreadful failure
to perceive the cloth as yellow is the result
of a tacit assumption by the brain concerning
the constancy of the physical characteristics
of all things including tablecloths, candles
and dancers.

DIFFERENT AVENUE

What is this world coming to?
Dancers dressed in sacks and tents,
stretch garments and hoods to hide
the fact that we are watching people dance.
The nerve of such choreographers.
Would they admit that they do not care
for us or dancers or humanity?
Why do they hide human bodies?
Then one night, leaving a theatre,
we paused. Something had occurred.
We'd seen no toes, no hair, no ankles, no eyes,
no calves, no shoulders, no knees, no arms,
no legs, no hands, no thighs or tummies,
never an odd or funny place banned by church
and state and all decent minded folk.
We walked off into the night knowing
we had become aware, despite our years
of enjoying ohhh! so much dance,
that we'd become aware of motion and form.
Motion and form for their own reasons to be.
Yes, we saw the forms of motion.

IDOLIZING

Ridiculous legend and goofy story 'bout fame
pass to us from scores and centuries past.
Dancers, persons turned technical wizards,
special souls unveiling unusual states,
people of unique gesture or mime or movement,
they appeared on prints. One dancer's likeness
was formed by a confectioner into candy statuettes.
Boats and horses were named in their fame.
Shops were stocked with undergarments, footwear,
boot polish, shaving soap, even cigars
bearing their names.
Far far out?
Fans of one queen of dance
carrying their love to such extreme,
they arranged a rare banquet date
just to show what fans can mean.
They chewed and chewed and chewed and ate.
So there they were as if at meat.
Cooked and served in sauce superb
a pair of the lady's dance shoes
honestly!
heartily they did eat.

DANCER

Symmetrical pirouettes,
inspiring grand jetés,
a dance step is a dance step,
not a promise.
The dancer arrives today
as a new cultural hero
free of language, absent from politics,
devoid of the jargon of symposia,
academia, law courts and atomic threats.
There's nothing to discuss, only wisdom
of the body and endeavors kinetically done.
We seek the ultra rarity of people
holding a share of charisma and essence.
Somebody transfigures into an aesthetic object
radiating rhythm, line, balance and form.
Somewhere among us at the washing machines,
on the airliner, buying vegetables in the market,
or just walking down the street is one of us
who is a motion away from becoming
an objet d'art. Look sideways!
She or he may be that one, someone who'll
transport you to kinesthetic states
beyond your means.

BEING

From the nation of . . .
born . . .
daughter of . . .
she is currently the youngest
ballerina of the company.
She entered the school in . . .
and was graduated from it . . . .
She had a most unusual debut.
At the time when most of their
ballerinas were touring the U.S.,
she was entrusted with the role of . . .
while technically still a pupil.
She danced it with great success
for the first time . . . ,
breaking a record both in history
of the school and the theatre.
From . . . , her teacher, she acquired
grace and a strong technique.
Since graduating into the company
she has worked with . . . , who has passed
on to her her famous plasticity of arms
and nobility of manner, good line, musicality,
taste, and good extensions although she lacks
natural élévation and is a somewhat . . .

CURRENT EVENTS

What are the limits of a theatrical dancer?
That question we would ask also of art objects.
Aestheticians and critics noted decades ago
the use of strange materials and found objects.
Junkyards and basements rendered their forgotten items.
Artists plundered trash bins for treasures of cloth,
cans and bottles, paper and tin, rags and whatever.
Composers ransacked the world of sounds and noises
for crashes and bangs and scrapes,
screeches and roars and falling things,
chirps and burps and woodpeckers pecking.
Common objects and readymades of every kind
haunted the galleries with their cheap smugness.
They, no longer common things, did not fall backward
into their former banality. They became art.
Museums and theatres and galleries were sworn
to protect their wards from outside threats.
The sense and logic of the real world
gave way to an autonomy of a subculture.
The outer monarch was replaced by an inner code
of aesthetic theory empowering worlds of art.
Unusual dancers now have room to dance
in the roominess of current aesthetic space.
Art objects and dancers together share a climate.

CURTAIN

Magic of a dance theatre presents
a world in front of a world.
Behind those curtains wings frame a stage.
Air is brittle with uncertainties.
The curtain remains down.
Electric lines and poles with stark lights
challenge dancers to dance through obstacles
as heavy things hang high above their heads.
Kindly stay clear. A dancer is warming up.
There's a spin,
a turn,
a whipping leg,
a moment's pause.
Time to remove the leg warmers.
The curtain remains down.
On the other side spectators eagerly enter the theatre.
They possess admiring hearts yet wear critical eyes.
That dancer who becomes a great performer
consummates a purpose for living.
But a further phase stays in the offing,
that we might watch that moving spirit
to perceive the dancing aesthetic object.
Will it happen tonight?
The curtain is still down.

PARTNERING

He was asked to partner a girl whose mom
ran a big ballet school west of Chicago
where twice yearly all the town watched
a leading dancer, the school owner's daughter.
This young dancer was a stick thin
calm and lovely little lass
with perfect teeth and timid manner
no doubt brought on by that harsh
but great teacher and demon of a mom
who'd been, moons ago, one big New York dancer.
Of the dancing daughter he tells us
he groaned after her, he made
flirtatious eyes at her, he'd wriggle
in torture of desire when anywhere near.
She was a joy to behold in her tutu,
something from a lithograph when sur les pointes.
But as a ballet partner . . . . !
For her he'd begin rehearsals with caution
like a well seasoned soldier in combat.
She, a lovely gentle little lass,
during moments of dance became the menace
to his life and body and limbs.
Quite gracefully she poked fingers in eyes,
knees in groins, toes into stomachs,
and with all good intention as well
transformed simple lifts into superb disaster.
Ah, but he remembers with sweet favor

a slight and sinewy girl with goopie
pimples on her odd and homely face.
Though young she bore the vile voice
of a mid aged shrew, and he
never could stand to be near
when the dance was not theirs to share.
But as a ballet partner . . . . !

INJURY

Creatures clad in leotards and tights
bending across wood floors in studios . . .
The ticket was rather matter-of-factual.
It was headed with the name of the place.
It stated the dance company.
It noted: Tuesday evening,
8:00 P.M., no seating during performance,
March 1, 1997, admit one, $12.00,
no refunds or exchanges.
Creatures clad in leotards and tights
bending across wood floors in studios . . .
That leg was wrapped and packed in ice.
We lamented at her bedside.
She lay there devastated, her fair skin
turned pale from confinement, her hair
spread over the pillow, her eyes
staring beyond as if she were asking,
"Will I ever dance again?"
That leg was wrapped and packed in ice.
She turned the red brownish ticket
on its side. RIGHT A 30
BALCONY SIDES, but she waited
outside the stage door.
A leg stuck out from under some covers.
The leg was propped on several pillows.
That leg was wrapped and packed in ice.
A drab, drab, drab day for sure.

A little dancer months later
moving to the front of a swift ensemble
spun vibrant chains of pirouettes. She.
Creatures clad in leotards and tights
bending across wood floors in studios
remain beings from our world
but in the dance may become
works of art.

SHOW ME

Exhibit this hour's mood,
      dear dancer.
You seem reserved.

Go on, go on to reveal it.
How about it?
Perhaps you feel
elegant,
lofty,
aloof.
Please express it.
Avoid joining me. I will watch.

Go ahead, put a strong leg forward.
Throw the other behind you.
Raise it high behind you.
Bend that back knee sharply,
keep your foot just below it.
Raise high that back arm.
Beautifully curve it toward its own hand.
Stretch that other arm to the side.
Hey! Watch those shoulders.
Keep 'em down.
That's good. You're looking good.
Now lean a bit forward,
toward that supporting leg,
and arch your back, arch it well.

Your head. It stares stupidly nowhere.
Might you wish to look with inspiration
up, back up at your raised palm?
Or would you be so demure
to turn your eyes the other way
down at your extended lower arm?
Avoid joining me. I'll watch.
Easy does it . . . . . easy.
I see what you're doing.
Go on if you will,
rise up on the front leg.
Try the half point. Try it.
Careful, careful, careful.
Keep that leg turned out.
Keep it firm. Keep it straight.
No, no, don't get mushy.
Tighten those ass muscles,
your thighs, your gut.
Tension. Tension.
You're doing well.
Try holding it.
Not bad.
Not too bad.
O.K.
Whooooops . . .
Your balance . . . . what happened?
You were doing fine.
Shall we start again?
Avoid joining me. Certainly I will watch.

TOUCHING

Look over there. See that painting.
How strongly it invites our glance.
We look intently into its regions
sporting bright vast textural life.
Thick pigments so highly raised,
strokes expanding three dimensions,
patches jutting jaggedly out,
portions impudently wandering about
and circular areas reaching to us.
This is not unlike the dancing dancer.
Then we make our error,
an error that brings us out of a garden
back into the screaming light of commonplaces.
We approach to touch the work,
the cold hard stinky prickly paint
slapped on swaying cloth.
Visions down, zeal down, delight down.
Some chagrin and surprise.
We touched the sweating dancer.
We're blown away by a mouth of heavy
pulsating vapor and that banality
of exhausted limbs which we'd find
exercising at playgrounds and gyms.
The dancer changed from sight supreme
to commonplace human being.
The line, the form, the colors, the painting
all turned from glories perceived
to bodily stuff.

THE AUTHOR has organized public readings by contemporary poets and discussions on criticism by current writers. He has also given talks on dance history, hosted ensemble demonstrations, and written articles. His book length works include

Dancer and Spectator: An Aesthetic Distance

La danse aux Etats-Unis

Tanz jeder Art in USA

Dancer and Other Aesthetic Objects

and this unique collection of his poetry

Dancers Are Poems